Bible Promises for New Parents

Presented to *Erica & Josh*

Given by *Great Grandfather Frank & Great Grandmother Betty With God's blessings and our love —*

Date *January 19, 2008*

Raquel Lynn Winterburn

T hat they and their children
will prosper forever.

Deuteronomy 5:29

Bible Promises for New Parents

BROADMAN
& HOLMAN
PUBLISHERS

Nashville, Tennessee

Contents

Promises to Start With

Becoming a parent changes everything, they always say. And that's true in many ways. Yet at the same time, your passage into parenthood is another step in a long line of things God has been doing in your life over the years. All the experiences you've been accumulating are meeting in the middle of this incredible moment.

Yes, parenthood will make you a new person, but your deepest needs are still the same: your need for God's love, your need for His strength, your need for His promises.

The Gift of Children

What a Treasure I Have Been Given

Unless you are converted and become like children, you will never enter the kingdom of heaven. Therefore, whoever humbles himself like this child—this one is the greatest in the kingdom of heaven. And whoever welcomes one child like this in My name welcomes Me.

Matthew 18:3-5

Let your father and mother have joy, and let her who gave birth to you rejoice.

Proverbs 23:25

Even a sparrow finds a home, and a swallow, a nest for herself where she places her young— near Your altars, LORD of Hosts, my King and my God.

Psalm 84:3

Sons are indeed a heritage from the LORD, children, a reward. Like arrows in the hand of a warrior are the sons born in one's youth. Happy is the man who has filled his quiver with them. Such men will never be put to shame when they speak with their enemies at the city gate.

Psalm 127:3-5

You will eat there in the presence of the LORD your God, and rejoice with your household in everything you do.

Deuteronomy 12:7

**God gives us many blessings in life.
Children are among His very finest.**
*We are cared for so completely by our heavenly
Father. And how gracious of Him to even meet
our need for someone so small, so precious to love.*

All these blessings will come and overtake
you, because you obey the LORD your God:
You will be blessed in the city and blessed in
the country. Your descendants will be blessed,
and your soil's produce, and the offspring of
your livestock, including the young of your
herds and the newborn of your flocks. Your
basket and kneading bowl will be blessed.
You will be blessed when you come in
and blessed when you go out.

Deuteronomy 28:2-6

He protects his flock like a shepherd; He
gathers the lambs in His arms, and carries
them in the fold of His garment.

Isaiah 40:11a

The Gift of Children

Children were brought to Him so He might put His hands on them and pray. But the disciples rebuked them. Then Jesus said, "Leave the children alone, and don't try to keep them from coming to Me, because the kingdom of heaven is made up of people like this."

Matthew 19:13-14

In the fear of the LORD one has strong confidence and his children have a refuge.

Proverbs 14:26

He gives the childless woman a household, making her the joyful mother of children.

Psalm 113:9

See that you don't look down on one of these little ones, because I tell you that in heaven their angels continually view the face of My Father in heaven. For the Son of Man has come to save the lost.

What do you think? If a man has 100 sheep, and one of them goes astray, won't he leave the 99 on the hillside, and go and search for the stray? And if he finds it, I assure you: He rejoices over that sheep more than over the 99 that did not go astray.

In the same way, it is not the will of your Father in heaven that one of these little ones perish.

Matthew 18:10-14

The Gift of Children

Your Father has such great love for your children . . . and also for you.
The relationship you are beginning to enjoy with your child gives you keen insight into God's love. This Father of yours will always be true to you.

Fathers, don't stir up anger in your children, but bring them up in the training and instruction of the Lord.

Ephesians 6:4

For I have chosen him so that he will command his children and his house after him to keep the way of the LORD by doing what is right and just.

Genesis 18:19

For children are not obligated to save up for their parents, but parents for their children. I will most gladly spend and be spent for you.

2 Corinthians 12:14-15

The Fatherhood of God

Show Me What a Parent Should Be

What man among you, if his son asks him for bread, will give him a stone? Or if he asks for a fish, will give him a snake? If you then, who are evil, know how to give good gifts to your children, how much more will your Father in heaven give good things to those who ask!

Matthew 7:9-11

As a father has compassion on his children, so the LORD has compassion on those who fear Him. For He knows what we are made of, remembering that we are dust.

Psalm 103:13-14

For this reason I bow my knees before the Father from whom every family in heaven and on earth is named.

Ephesians 3:14-15

From one man He has made every nation of men to live all over the earth and has determined their appointed times and the boundaries of where they live, so that they might seek God, and perhaps they might reach out and find Him, though He is not far from each one of us. For in Him we live and move and exist.

Acts 17:26-28

For us there is one God, the Father, from whom are all things, and we for Him.

1 Corinthians 8:6

In the face of God, we see a Father who loves us just for who we are.
It's not merely a feeling, but a love that expresses itself in total commitment. He will never fail His children. And likewise, we must never fail ours.

Look at how great a love the Father has given us, that we should be called God's children. And we are!

1 John 3:1

Look at the birds of the sky: they don't sow or reap or gather into barns, yet your heavenly Father feeds them. Aren't you worth more than they?

Matthew 6:26

We are the clay, and You are our potter.

Isaiah 64:8

You, LORD, are our Father; from ancient times, Your name is our Redeemer.

Isaiah 63:16

The Fatherhood of God

I will be a Father to you, and you will be sons and daughters to Me, says the Lord Almighty.

2 Corinthians 6:18

Dear friends, we are God's children now, and what we will be has not yet been revealed. We know that when He appears, we will be like Him, because we will see Him as He is. And everyone who has this hope in Him purifies himself just as He is pure.

1 John 3:2-3

Be perfect, therefore, as your heavenly Father is perfect.

Matthew 5:48

Do not take the Lord's discipline lightly, or faint when you are reproved by Him; for the Lord disciplines the one He loves, and punishes every son whom He receives.

Endure it as discipline: God is dealing with you as sons. For what son is there whom a father does not discipline? But if you are without discipline—which all receive—then you are illegitimate children and not sons.

Furthermore, we had natural fathers discipline us, and we respected them. Shouldn't we submit even more to the Father of spirits and live? For they disciplined us for a short time based on what seemed good to them, but He does it for our benefit, so that we can share His holiness.

Hebrews 12:5-10

**He gives His gifts to us fully, freely—
for our own good, for His own glory.**
*You will be doing most of the giving in these early
stages of your child's life. You will be an example
of the One who never stops caring for His kids.*

Every generous act and every perfect gift is
from above, coming down from the Father of
lights; with Him there is no variation or shadow
cast by turning.

James 1:17

Don't be afraid, little flock, because your
Father delights to give you the kingdom.

Luke 12:32

So don't be foolish, but understand what the
Lord's will is. . . . speaking to one another in
psalms, hymns, and spiritual songs, singing
and making music to the Lord in your heart,
giving thanks always for everything to God the
Father in the name of our Lord Jesus Christ.

Ephesians 5:17, 19-20

The Essence of Trust

This Job Is Much Bigger Than I Am

Remain in Me, and I in you. Just as a branch is unable to produce fruit by itself unless it remains on the vine, so neither can you unless you remain in Me. I am the vine; you are the branches. The one who remains in Me and I in him produces much fruit, because you can do nothing without Me.

John 15:4-5

We have this kind of confidence toward God through Christ: not that we are competent in ourselves to consider anything as coming from ourselves, but our competence is from God.

2 Corinthians 3:4-5

He is not impressed by the strength of a horse; He does not value the power of a man. The LORD values those who fear Him, those who hope in His faithful love.

Psalm 147:10-11

Trust in the LORD with all your heart, and do not rely on your own understanding; think about Him in all your ways, and He will guide you on the right paths.

Proverbs 3:5-6

Blessed is the person who trusts in the LORD, whose trust indeed is the LORD.

Jeremiah 17:7

For You are their magnificent strength.

Psalm 89:17

You life has been a practice in trust— a trust you need now more than ever.
One of the reasons God was there to take care of you through your early years was to assure you He could still do it when the stakes got this high.

You took me from the womb, making me secure while at my mother's breast. I was given over to You at birth; You have been my God from my mother's womb.

Psalm 22:9-10

For You are my hope, Lord GOD, my confidence from my youth. I have leaned on You from birth; You took me from my mother's womb. My praise is always about You.

Psalm 71:5-6

Whom do I have in heaven but You? And I desire nothing on earth but You. My flesh and my heart may fail, but God is the strength of my heart, my portion forever.

Psalm 73:25-26

The Essence of Trust

I call to You from the ends of the earth when my heart is without strength. Lead me to a rock that is high above me. . . . Then I will continually sing of Your name, fulfilling my vows day by day.

Psalm 61:2, 8

Those who know Your name trust in You because You have not abandoned those who seek You, LORD.

Psalm 9:10

You will keep in perfect peace the mind that is dependent on You, for it is trusting in You.

Isaiah 26:3

Now, this is what the LORD says—the One who created you, Jacob, and the One who formed you, Israel—"Do not fear, for I have redeemed you; I have called you by your name; you are Mine.

"I will be with you when you pass through the waters, and when you pass through the rivers, they will not overwhelm you. You will not be burned when you walk through the fire, and the flame will not burn you.

"For I am the LORD your God, the Holy One of Israel, your Savior."

Isaiah 43:1-3

**You have strength available to you
that no difficulty can ever outmatch.**
*So take comfort in the incredible, sustaining
power of God. He already has your child's future
under total control . . . and you under His wing.*

So because of Christ, I am pleased in
weaknesses. . . . For when I am weak, then
I am strong.

2 Corinthians 12:10

God's foolishness is wiser than human wisdom, and God's weakness is stronger than
human strength.

1 Corinthians 1:25

Lord GOD, You indeed are God; Your words
are true, and You have promised this good
thing to Your servant. So now, may it please
You to bless Your servant's house that it may
continue before You forever. For You, Lord
GOD, have spoken, and with Your blessing
Your servant's house will be blessed forever.

2 Samuel 7:28-29

The Challenges of Change

Now for Something Completely Different

I know both how to have a little, and I know how to have a lot. In any and all circumstances I have learned the secret of being content— whether well-fed or hungry, whether in abundance or in need. I am able to do all things through Him who strengthens me.

Philippians 4:12-13

Everything has its appointed hour,
every matter its time under the heavens.

Ecclesiastes 3:1

A man's heart plans his way, but the LORD determines his steps.

Proverbs 16:9

I am sure of this, that He who started a good work in you will carry it on to completion until the day of Christ Jesus.

Philippians 1:6

Don't worry about anything, but in everything, through prayer and petition with thanksgiving, let your requests be made known to God. And the peace of God, which surpasses every thought, will guard your hearts and your minds in Christ Jesus.

Philippians 4:6-7

The LORD bless you and protect you.

Numbers 6:24

**Yes, things are a lot different now.
But your need for God is still the same.**
*The changes that arise when a new baby's in the
house are simply fresh opportunities to grow, to
learn, to look to your Father for everything.*

We are asking that you may be filled with the
knowledge of His will in all wisdom and spiritual understanding, so that you may walk worthy of the Lord, fully pleasing to Him, bearing
fruit in every good work and growing in the
knowledge of God. May you be strengthened
with all power, according to His glorious might,
for all endurance and patience, with joy giving
thanks to the Father, who has enabled you to
share in the saints' inheritance in the light.

Colossians 1:9-12

For His divine power has given us everything
required for life and godliness, through the
knowledge of Him who called us by His
own glory and goodness.

2 Peter 1:3

Let Your work be seen by Your servants, and Your splendor by their children. Let the favor of the Lord our God be upon us; establish for us the work of our hands—establish the work of our hands!

Psalm 90:16-17

When you walk, your steps will not be hindered; when you run, you will not stumble.

Proverbs 4:12

And whatever you do, in word or in deed, do everything in the name of the Lord Jesus, giving thanks to God the Father through Him.

Colossians 3:17

Lord, You have searched me and known me. You know when I sit down and when I stand up; You understand my thoughts from far away.

You observe my travels and my rest; You are aware of all my ways. Before a word is on my tongue, You know all about it, Lord. You have encircled me; You have placed Your hand on me. This extraordinary knowledge is beyond me. It is lofty; I am unable to reach it. . . .

If I live at the eastern horizon or settle at the western limits, even there Your hand will lead me; Your right hand will hold on to me.

Psalm 139:1-6, 9-10

The more things change, the more the really important things stay the same. *So keep seeking God, keep worshiping Him for His power and strength, keep seeing each day for what it is—another chance to live as His child.*

This is the day the LORD has made; let us rejoice and be glad in it.

Psalm 118:24

A man's steps are established by the LORD, and He takes pleasure in his way.

Psalm 37:23

Jesus Christ is the same yesterday, today, and forever.

Hebrews 13:8

Be clear-headed and disciplined for prayer. Above all, keep your love for one another at full strength.

1 Peter 4:7-8

The Pursuit of Godliness

This Is a Good Time to Get Serious

And in view of this, we always pray for you that our God will consider you worthy of His calling, and will—by His power—fulfill every desire for goodness and the work of faith, so that the name of our Lord Jesus will be glorified by you, and you by Him.

2 Thessalonians 1:11-12

When all has been heard, the conclusion of the matter is this: fear God and obey His commandments, because this is all there is to being human.

Ecclesiastes 12:13

What does the LORD your God ask of you except to fear the LORD your God by walking in all His ways, to love Him, and to serve the LORD your God with all your heart and all your soul?

Deuteronomy 10:12

Not that I have already reached the goal or am already fully mature, but I make every effort to take hold of it because I also have been taken hold of by Christ Jesus.

Brothers, I do not consider myself to have taken hold of it. But one thing I do: forgetting what is behind and reaching forward to what is ahead, I pursue as my goal the prize promised by God's heavenly call in Christ Jesus.

Philippians 3:12-14

There's someone new who's watching every little thing you do. Are you?
Our responsibility for serving God turns up a notch when one so young and observant is in our care. They deserve from us our finest obedience.

You are the light of the world. A city situated on a hill cannot be hidden. No one lights a lamp and puts it under a basket, but rather on a lampstand, and it gives light for all who are in the house. In the same way, let your light shine before men, so that they may see your good works and give glory to your Father in heaven.
Matthew 5:14-16

Practice these things; be committed to them, so that your progress may be evident to all.
1 Timothy 4:15

Commit your way to the LORD; trust in Him, and He will act, making your righteousness shine like the dawn, your justice like the noonday.
Psalm 37:5-6

Therefore as you have received Christ Jesus the Lord, walk in Him, rooted and built up in Him and established in the faith, just as you were taught, and overflowing with thankfulness.

Colossians 2:6-7

For you were once darkness, but now you are light in the Lord. Walk as children of light— for the fruit of the light results in all goodness, righteousness, and truth—discerning what is pleasing to the Lord.

Ephesians 5:8-10

May He give you what your heart desires.

Psalm 20:4

Make every effort to supplement your faith with goodness, goodness with knowledge, knowledge with self-control, self-control with endurance, endurance with godliness, godliness with brotherly affection, and brotherly affection with love. For if these qualities are yours and are increasing, they will keep you from being useless or unfruitful in the knowledge of our Lord Jesus Christ. . . .

Therefore, brothers, make every effort to confirm your calling and election, because if you do these things you will never stumble. For in this way, entry into the eternal kingdom of our Lord and Savior Jesus Christ will be richly supplied to you.

2 Peter 1:5-8, 10-11

Living for God is more a matter of submission to Him than fighting sin.
Turning over your life to Christ as Lord of your life doesn't cost nearly as much as it pays. Being in His will is better than anything life has to offer.

I will live with integrity of heart in my house. I will not set anything godless before my eyes.

Psalm 101:2-3

Therefore, submit to God. But resist the Devil, and he will flee from you. Draw near to God, and He will draw near to you.

James 4:7-8

Let all who seek You rejoice and be glad in You; let those who love Your salvation continually say, "Great is the LORD!"

Psalm 40:16

For me, living is Christ.

Philippians 1:21

Promises to Grow On

Bringing a new baby into the house brightens your home with smiles and soft colors. It means you hear cooing where there used to be quiet— the feel of a soft blanket on your shoulder, the sound of steady breathing, and the just-right weight of your child in your arms.

Of course, it also means you'll be seeing a lot more of the middle of the night. You'll be busy and bleary-eyed and border on exhaustion.

New parenthood is all these things rolled into one—and a great place to learn about God.

Enjoying the Newness

I've Never Felt Quite This Way Before

How great is Your goodness that You have stored up for those who fear You, and accomplished in the sight of everyone for those who take refuge in You. . . . May the LORD be praised, for He has wonderfully shown His faithful love to me.

Psalm 31:19, 21

Sing a new song to the LORD, for He has performed wonders.

Psalm 98:1

He put a new song in my mouth, a hymn of praise to our God.

Psalm 40:3

Our mouths were filled with laughter then, and our tongues with shouts of joy. Then they said among the nations, "The LORD has done great things for them." The LORD had done great things for us; we were joyful.

Psalm 126:2-3

The LORD's works are great, studied by all who delight in them. All that He does is splendid and majestic; His righteousness endures forever.

Psalm 111:2-3

His compassions have no end. They are new every morning; great is Your faithfulness.

Lamentations 3:22-23

The wonder of life is beyond words to describe it. All you can do is worship.
This child you hold in your arms is a miraculous gift from God. Every time you look into that little face, see a big God who can do incredible things.

LORD, I have heard the report about You; I stand in awe, O LORD, of Your deeds. In these years revive Your work; in these years make it known.

Habakkuk 3:2

Then our sons will be like plants nurtured in their youth; our daughters, like corner pillars that are carved in the palace style. Our storehouses will be full, supplying all kinds of produce; our flocks will increase by thousands and tens of thousands in our open fields. . . . Happy are the people with such blessings. Happy are the people whose God is the LORD.

Psalm 144:12-13, 15

I will praise You because I am unique in remarkable ways. Your works are wonderful, and I know this very well. My bones were not hidden from You when I was made in secret, when I was formed in the depths of the earth. Your eyes saw me when I was formless; all my days were written in Your book and planned before a single one of them began. God, how difficult Your thoughts are for me to comprehend; how vast their sum is!

Psalm 139:14-17

My heart revels in the LORD; my strength is exalted in the LORD.

1 Samuel 2:1

How countless are Your works, LORD!
In wisdom You have made them all; the earth
is full of Your creatures. Here is the sea, vast
and wide, teeming with creatures beyond num-
ber—living things both large and small. There
the ships move about, and Leviathan, which
You formed to play there.

All of them wait for You to give them their
food at the right time. When You give it to
them, they gather it; when You open Your
hand, they are satisfied with good things. . . .
When You send Your breath, they are created,
and You renew the face of the earth.

Psalm 104:24-28, 30

New birth is a picture of what God does in our hearts. Celebrate His love.
You are as precious in your Father's eyes as this newborn baby is in yours. When God restored your soul, He made you a whole new creation.

Blessed be the God and Father of our Lord Jesus Christ. According to His great mercy, He has given us a new birth into a living hope through the resurrection of Jesus Christ from the dead, and into an inheritance that is imperishable, uncorrupted, and unfading, kept in heaven for you, who are being protected by God's power through faith for a salvation that is ready to be revealed in the last time.

1 Peter 1:3-5

My soul, praise the LORD, and all that is within me, praise His holy name. My soul, praise the LORD, and do not forget all His benefits. . . . He satisfies you with goodness; your youth is renewed like the eagle.

Psalm 103:1-2, 5

Needing Each Other

Man and Wife, Now More Than Ever

The man said: "This one, at last, is bone of my bone, and flesh of my flesh; this one will be called woman, for she was taken from man." This is why a man leaves his father and mother and bonds with his wife, and they become one flesh.

Genesis 2:23-24

Haven't you read," [Jesus] replied, "that He who created them in the beginning 'made them male and female', and He also said: 'For this reason a man will leave his father and mother and be joined to his wife, and the two will become one flesh?' So they are no longer two, but one flesh. Therefore what God has joined together, man must not separate."

Matthew 19:4-6

Love's flames are fiery flames—the fiercest of all. Mighty waters cannot extinguish love; rivers cannot sweep it away.

Song of Songs 8:6-7

Let me see your face; let me hear your voice.

Song of Songs 2:14

My love is mine and I am his.

Song of Songs 2:16

This is my love, and this is my friend.

Song of Songs 5:16

**Love your child—oh, love your child—
but don't forget to love each other.**
*The bond you share in marriage is not only a gift
you give yourselves but also a gift you give to your
children. They need you to need one another.*

A house and wealth are inherited from fathers,
but a sensible wife is from the LORD.

Proverbs 19:14

Husbands, love your wives, just as also Christ
loved the church and gave Himself for her, to
make her holy, cleansing her in the washing of
water by the word. He did this to present the
church to Himself in splendor, without spot
or wrinkle or any such thing, but holy and
blameless.

Ephesians 5:25-27

With all humility and gentleness, with patience, accepting one another in love, diligently
keeping the unity of the Spirit.

Ephesians 4:2-3

Needing Each Other

A man who finds a wife finds a good thing
and obtains favor from the LORD.

Proverbs 18:22

Her sons rise up and call her blessed. Her
husband also praises her: "Many women are
capable, but you surpass them all!" Charm is
deceptive and beauty is fleeting, but a woman
who fears the LORD will be praised. Give her
the reward of her labor, and let her works
praise her at the city gates.

Proverbs 31:28-31

A capable wife is her husband's crown.

Proverbs 12:4

Husbands should love their wives as their own bodies. He who loves his wife loves himself. For no one ever hates his own flesh, but provides and cares for it, just as Christ does for the church, since we are members of His body.

"For this reason a man will leave his father and mother and be joined to his wife, and the two will become one flesh."

This mystery is profound, but I am talking about Christ and the church. To sum up, each one of you is to love his wife as himself, and the wife is to respect her husband.

Ephesians 5:28-33

Your lives just became more complex. So keep your love pure and simple.
Shower affection on your wife, your husband.
Remember the love that first drew you together.
Kindle the love that will keep you that way.

It is not good for the man to be alone.

Genesis 2:18

My love calls to me: "Arise, my darling. Come away, my beautiful one. For now the winter is past; the rain has ended and gone away. The blossoms appear in the countryside. The time of singing has come, and the turtledove's cooing is heard in our land. The fig tree ripens its figs; the blossoming vines give off their fragrance. Arise, my darling. Come away, my beautiful one."

Song of Songs 2:10-13

You have captured my heart with one glance of your eyes.

Song of Songs 4:9

Making Good Choices

I Want to Do This Right from the Start

He gives wisdom to the wise and knowledge to those who have understanding. He reveals the deep and hidden things; He knows what is in the darkness, and light dwells with Him. I offer thanks and praise to You, God of my fathers, because You have given me wisdom.

Daniel 2:21-23

Now if any of you lacks wisdom, he should ask God, who gives to all generously and without criticizing, and it will be given to him.

But let him ask in faith without doubting. For the doubter is like the surging sea, driven and tossed by the wind. That person should not expect to receive anything from the Lord.

James 1:5-7

Hold on to instruction; don't let go. Guard it, for it is your life.

Proverbs 4:13

Then you will understand righteousness, justice, and integrity—every good path. For wisdom will enter your heart, and knowledge will delight your soul. Discretion will watch over you, and understanding will guard you, rescuing you from the way of evil—from the one who says perverse things, from those who abandon the right paths to walk in ways of darkness.

Proverbs 2:9-13

You do have big decisions to make. But you have a big God to help you.

The secret to making wise choices concerning your family and your future doesn't require that you know everything, but that you know Who does.

The fear of the LORD is the beginning of wisdom; all who follow His instructions have good insight.

Psalm 111:10

The fear of the LORD is wisdom's instruction, and humility comes before honor.

Proverbs 15:33

I love those who love me, and those who search for me find me. With me are riches and honor, lasting wealth and righteousness. My fruit is better than solid gold, and my harvest than pure silver. I walk in the way of righteousness, along the paths of justice, giving wealth as an inheritance to those who love me, and filling their treasuries.

Proverbs 8:17-21

Making Good Choices

But be doers of the word and not hearers only, deceiving yourselves. Because if anyone is a hearer of the word and not a doer, he is like a man looking at his own face in a mirror; for he looks at himself, goes away, and right away forgets what kind of man he was.

But the one who looks intently into the perfect law of freedom and perseveres in it, and is not a forgetful hearer but a doer who acts—this person will be blessed in what he does.

James 1:22-25

The Spirit of the LORD will rest on Him—a Spirit of wisdom and understanding, a Spirit of counsel and strength, a Spirit of knowledge and of the fear of the LORD.

Isaiah 11:2

If you accept my words and store up my commands within you, listening closely to wisdom and directing your heart to understanding; furthermore, if you call out to insight and lift your voice to understanding, if you seek it like silver and search for it like hidden treasure, then you will understand the fear of the LORD and discover the knowledge of God.

For the LORD gives wisdom; from His mouth come knowledge and understanding. He stores up success for the upright; He is a shield for those who live with integrity so that He may guard the paths of justice and protect the way of His loyal followers.

Proverbs 2:1-8

Everyone is usually willing to share their opinion, but only God's matters.
You'll be tempted to model your family after the mold and expectations of those around you. Make sure your goals are grounded in the Word of God.

Pay careful attention, then, to how you walk—not as unwise people but as wise—making the most of the time, because the days are evil.

Ephesians 5:15-16

Do not be conformed to this age, but be transformed by the renewing of your mind, so that you may discern what is the good, pleasing, and perfect will of God.

Romans 12:2

This also comes from the LORD of Hosts. He gives wonderful advice; He gives great wisdom.

Isaiah 28:29

Keeping your Balance

I Know I Can't Do Everything

Come to Me, all you who are weary and burdened, and I will give you rest. Take My yoke upon you and learn from Me, because I am gentle and humble in heart, and you will find rest for your souls. For My yoke is easy and My burden is light.

Matthew 11:28-30

Don't worry about your life, what you will eat or what you will drink; or about your body, what you will wear. Isn't life more than food and the body more than clothing?

Matthew 6:25

The LORD is my shepherd; there is nothing I lack. He lets me lie down in green pastures; He leads me beside quiet waters. He renews my life; He leads me along the right paths for His name's sake.

Psalm 23:1-3

He will stand and shepherd them in the strength of the LORD, in the majestic name of the LORD His God. They will live securely, for at that time His greatness will extend to the ends of the earth. This One will be the source of peace.

Micah 5:4-5

For He Himself has said, "I will never leave you or forsake you."

Hebrews 13:5

Yes, being a parent is a tough job, but you can do it, okay? You can do it. *It's one day at a time, making memories with every moment, relying on God to keep you alert, not bogged down in doing things that can wait.*

This is what the LORD says, "Stand by the roadways and look. Ask about the ancient paths, where the good way to good is, then walk on it and find rest for yourselves.

Jeremiah 6:16

The result of righteousness will be peace; the effect of righteousness will be quiet confidence forever. Then My people will dwell in a peaceful place, and in safe and restful dwellings.

Isaiah 32:17-18

Come, let us worship and bow down; let us kneel before the LORD our Maker. For He is our God, and we are the people of His pasture, the sheep under His care.

Psalm 95:6-7

LORD, You are my portion and my cup of blessing; You hold my future. The boundary lines have fallen for me in pleasant places; indeed, I have a beautiful inheritance.

Psalm 16:5-6

If I say, "My foot is slipping," Your faithful love will support me, LORD. When I am filled with cares, Your comfort brings me joy.

Psalm 94:18-19

The LORD is good to those who hope in Him—to the one who seeks Him. It is good for one to wait silently for the LORD's salvation.

Lamentations 3:25-26

What profit does the worker gain when he struggles? I see the business that God gives people to keep them busy. He has arranged everything appropriately in its time and has also put forever in their hearts.

Still no one can discover the accomplishment God has accomplished from beginning to end.

I know nothing is better for anyone than to rejoice and to accomplish good with their lives. Also, it is God's gift whenever anyone eats, drinks, and experiences good in all his struggle.

Ecclesiastes 3:9-13

These are once-in-a-lifetime moments. Take them slowly; enjoy them together. *Your child will be six, then sixteen, soon enough. Treasure these times right now. Sure, you could keep yourself busy doing other things. But why?*

Lord, my heart is not proud; my eyes are not haughty. I do not get involved with things too great or too difficult for me. Instead, I have calmed and quieted myself like a little weaned child with its mother; I am like a little child.

Psalm 131:1-2

But we encourage you, brothers, to do so even more, to seek to lead a quiet life, to mind your own business, and to work with your own hands, as we commanded you.

1 Thessalonians 4:10-11

Therefore, whether you eat or drink, or whatever you do, do everything for God's glory.

1 Corinthians 10:31

Staying Up Late

Give Me Some Verses for the Wee Hours

I will lead the blind by a way they did not know; I will guide them on paths they have not known. I will turn darkness to light in front of them, and rough places into level ground. This is what I will do for them, and I will not forsake them.

Isaiah 42:16

It is good to praise the LORD, to sing praise to Your name, Most High, to declare Your faithful love in the morning and Your faithfulness at night.

Psalm 92:1-2

The LORD will send His faithful love by day; His song will be with me in the night— a prayer to the God of my life.

Psalm 42:8

Your statutes are the theme of my song during my earthly life. I remember Your name in the night, LORD, and I keep Your law. This is my practice: I obey Your precepts.

Psalm 119:54-56

For You, O LORD, are my lamp; the LORD illuminates my darkness.

2 Samuel 22:29

The day is Yours, also the night.

Psalm 74:16

Being called into action late at night can be both a chore . . . and a blessing.
While you're singing your little one back to sleep, you can be enjoying a side of worship you never knew before—the after-hours faithfulness of God.

The one who lives under the protection of the Most High dwells in the shadow of the Almighty.

Psalm 91:1

If I say, "Surely the darkness will hide me, and the light around me will become night"—even the darkness is not too dark for You. The night shines like the day; darkness and light are alike to You.

Psalm 139:11-12

I will praise the LORD who counsels me—even at night my conscience instructs me. I keep the LORD in mind always. Because He is at my right hand, I will not be defeated.

Psalm 16:7-8

Now praise the LORD, all you servants of the LORD who stand in the LORD's house at night! Lift up your hands in the holy place, and praise the LORD!

Psalm 134:1-2

The heavens declare the glory of God, and the sky proclaims the work of His hands. Day after day they pour out speech; night after night they communicate knowledge.

Psalm 19:1-2

Light shines in the darkness for the upright.

Psalm 112:4

I raise my eyes toward the mountains. Where will my help come from? My help comes from the LORD, the Maker of heaven and earth. He will not allow your foot to slip; your Protector will not slumber. Indeed, the Protector of Israel does not slumber or sleep.

The LORD protects you; the LORD is a shelter right by your side. The sun will not strike you by day, or the moon by night. The LORD will protect you from all harm; He will protect your life. The LORD will protect your coming and going both now and forever.

Psalm 121:1-8

It's when you're the most exhausted that God's strength can be the sweetest. *Go to sleep tonight knowing that if it's for two hours, four hours, six if you're lucky, your Father will be watching over your family all night long.*

When, on my bed, I think of You, I meditate on You during the night watches because You are my help; I will rejoice in the shadow of Your wings.

Psalm 63:6-7

I am awake through each watch of the night to meditate on Your promise.

Psalm 119:148

I lie down and sleep; I wake again because the LORD sustains me.

Psalm 3:5

Weeping may spend the night, but there is joy in the morning.

Psalm 30:5

Promises to Follow Through

You'll be so glad you found out about these promises now—while your child is still young, while your future is still before you, while the foundation of your family is still being formed and firmed up.

These promises of God that wrap themselves in prayer and worship, that surround you with the support of His church, that pick you up when you feel like packing it in, will become more than words in these special years. They'll become your assurance of a certain tomorrow.

In Need of Prayer

I Never Want to Leave Your Side

I love the LORD because He has heard my appeal for mercy. Because He has turned His ear to me, I will call out to Him as long as I live. . . . The LORD guards the inexperienced; I was helpless, and He saved me. Return to your rest, my soul, for the LORD has been good to you.

Psalm 116:1-2, 6-7

I call to You for help, LORD; in the morning my prayer meets You.

Psalm 88:13

At daybreak, LORD, You hear my voice; at daybreak I plead my case to You and watch expectantly.

Psalm 5:3

Let me experience Your faithful love in the morning, for I trust in You. Reveal to me the way I should go, because I long for You.

Psalm 143:8

May the LORD be praised, for He has heard the sound of my pleading. The LORD is my strength and my shield; my heart trusts in Him, and I am helped. Therefore my heart rejoices, and I praise Him with my song.

Psalm 28:6-7

Help us, O LORD our God, for we depend on You.

2 Chronicles 14:11

You're welcome anytime. Four in the morning. Ten at night. Any old time. *Prayer need not be long and formal. There are times and places for that, but also for prayer that's simply conversation, just between the two of you.*

I cry aloud to God, aloud to God, and He will hear me.

Psalm 77:1

If I had been aware of malice in my heart, the Lord would not have listened. However, God has listened; He has paid attention to the sound of my prayer. May God be praised! He has not turned away my prayer or turned His faithful love from me.

Psalm 66:18-20

Be gracious to me, Lord, for I call to You all day long. . . . I set my hope on You. For You, Lord, are kind and ready to forgive, abundant in faithful love to all who call on You.

Psalm 86:3-5

Therefore since we have a great high priest
who has passed through the heavens—Jesus the
Son of God—let us hold fast to the confession.
For we do not have a high priest who is unable
to sympathize with our weaknesses, but One
who has been tested in every way as we are,
yet without sin. Therefore let us approach the
throne of grace with boldness, so that we may
receive mercy and find grace to help us at the
proper time.

Hebrews 4:14-16

Because your Father knows the things you
need before you ask Him.

Matthew 6:8

You should pray like this:
  Our Father in heaven,
    Your name be honored as holy.
  Your kingdom come.
    Your will be done
    on earth as it is in heaven.
  Give us today our daily bread.
    And forgive us our debts,
    as we also have forgiven our debtors.
  And do not bring us into temptation,
    but deliver us from the evil one.
  For Yours is the kingdom and the power
    and the glory forever. Amen.

Matthew 6:9-13

In Need of Prayer

Prayer keeps you from feeling like you're having to do this all by yourself.
Sometimes we just require some reminding that God is as near as our next thought. Prayer keeps Him close to your daily work, your daily needs.

The LORD is near all who call out to Him, all who call out to Him with integrity. He fulfills the desires of those who fear Him; He hears their cry for help and saves them.

Psalm 145:18-19

Keep asking, and it will be given to you. Keep searching, and you will find. Keep knocking, and the door will be opened to you.

Matthew 7:7

Stay awake and pray, so that you won't enter into temptation. The spirit is willing, but the flesh is weak.

Matthew 26:41

Pray constantly.

1 Thessalonians 5:17

In Love with God

If I Ever Did Before, I Surely Do Now

Taste and see that the LORD is good. How happy is the man who takes refuge in Him! Fear the LORD, you His saints, for those who fear Him lack nothing. Young lions lack food and go hungry, but those who seek the LORD will not lack any good thing.

Psalm 34:8-10

Blessed be the God and Father of our Lord Jesus Christ, who has blessed us with every spiritual blessing in the heavens, in Christ.

Ephesians 1:3

You crown the year with Your goodness; Your ways overflow with plenty. The wilderness pastures overflow, and the hills are robed with joy. The pastures are clothed with flocks, and the valleys covered with grain. They shout in triumph; indeed, they sing.

Psalm 65:11-13

I will praise the LORD at all times; His praise will always be on my lips. I will boast in the LORD; the humble will hear and be glad.

Psalm 34:1-2

The LORD is the strength of His people; He is a stronghold of salvation for His anointed. Save Your people, bless Your possession, shepherd them, and carry them forever.

Psalm 28:8-9

Now that you're a parent, you have an extra special reason for loving God.
Imagine the blindness that must come over a person who can look into the face of one who's so precious and not love God a little bit more for it.

Lᴏʀᴅ, You have been our refuge in every generation. Before the mountains were born, before You gave birth to the earth and the world, from eternity to eternity, You are God.
Psalm 90:1-2

Bᴇtter a day in Your courts than a thousand anywhere else. I would rather be at the door of the house of my God than to live in the tents of the wicked.

Psalm 84:10

Iꜰ Your instruction had not been my delight, I would have died in my affliction. I will never forget Your precepts, for You have given me life through them.

Psalm 119:92-93

I remember the days of old; I meditate on all You have done; I reflect on the work of Your hands.

Psalm 143:5

You turned my lament into dancing; You removed my sackcloth and clothed me with gladness, so that I can sing to You and not be silent. LORD my God, I will praise You forever.

Psalm 30:11-12

My mouth will tell about Your righteousness and Your salvation all day long, though I cannot sum them up.

Psalm 71:15

Listen, Israel: The LORD our God, the LORD is One. Love the LORD your God with all your heart, with all your soul, and with all your strength.

These words that I am giving you today are to be in your heart. Repeat them to your children. Talk about them when you sit in your house and when you walk along the road, when you lie down and when you get up. Bind them as a sign on your hand and let them be a symbol on your forehead. Write them on the doorposts of your house and on your gates.

Deuteronomy 6:4-9

**Children give your worship a new set
of ears, a new impetus for your praise.**
*Your baby may not know what you're talking
about right now, but they'll learn to associate that
smile on your face with that Jesus in your heart.*

LORD, I love the house where You dwell, the
place where Your glory resides.

Psalm 26:8

Let the message about the Messiah dwell
richly among you, teaching and admonishing
one another in all wisdom, and singing psalms,
hymns, and spiritual songs, with gratitude in
your hearts to God.

Colossians 3:16

From the rising of the sun to its setting,
let the name of the LORD be praised.

Psalm 113:3

Let all who take refuge in You rejoice.

Psalm 5:11

In Community with Others

This Is Too Good to Keep to Yourself

Let us be concerned about one another
in order to promote love and good works,
not staying away from our meetings, as some
habitually do, but encouraging each other, and
all the more as you see the day drawing near.

Hebrews 10:24-25

How happy are those who reside in Your house, who praise You continually.

Psalm 84:4

Planted in the house of the LORD, they thrive in the courtyards of our God. They will still bear fruit in old age, healthy and green.

Psalm 92:13-14

So also you—since you are zealous in matters of the spirit, seek to excel in building up the church.

1 Corinthians 14:12

For you are all sons of God through faith in Christ Jesus. For as many of you as have been baptized into Christ have put on Christ. There is no Jew or Greek, slave or free, male or female; for you are all one in Christ Jesus.

Galatians 3:26-28

Therefore encourage one another and build each other up.

1 Thessalonians 5:11

Church may already be a big part of your life. It really needs to be one now. *This is not just Sunday morning stuff. This is a family that needs to serve you, that needs what your family can offer. This is the family of God.*

Now as we have many parts in one body, and all the parts do not have the same function, in the same way we who are many are one body in Christ and individually members of one another.

Romans 12:4-5

How good and pleasant it is when brothers can live together! . . . For there the LORD has appointed the blessing—life forevermore.

Psalm 133:1, 3

Therefore, as we have opportunity, we must work for the good of all, especially for those who belong to the household of faith.

Galatians 6:10

Based on the gift they have received, everyone should use it to serve others, as good managers of the varied grace of God.

If anyone speaks, his speech should be like the oracles of God; if anyone serves, his service should be from the strength God provides, so that in everything God may be glorified through Jesus Christ. To Him belong the glory and the power forever and ever. Amen.

1 Peter 4:10-11

Everyone should look out not only for his own interests, but also for the interests of others.

Philippians 2:4

When Christ came, He proclaimed the good news of peace to you who were far away and peace to those who were near. For through Him we both have access by one Spirit to the Father.

So then you are no longer foreigners and strangers, but fellow citizens with the saints, and members of God's household, built on the foundation of the apostles and prophets, with Christ Jesus Himself as the cornerstone. The whole building is being fitted together in Him and is growing into a holy sanctuary in the Lord, in whom you also are being built together for God's dwelling in the Spirit.

Ephesians 2:17-22

So make sure you have a church to call home, a place where you belong.
You need it, your marriage needs it, your new child needs it, you all need it. God's design is to put us in families, and also in families of faith.

I urge you, brothers, in the name of our Lord Jesus Christ, that you all say the same thing, that there be no divisions among you, and that you be united with the same understanding and the same conviction.

1 Corinthians 1:10

But encourage each other daily, while it is still called today, so that none of you is hardened by sin's deception. For we have become companions of the Messiah if we hold firmly until the end the reality that we had at the start.

Hebrews 3:13-14

Let us hold on to the confession of our hope without wavering, for He who promised is faithful.

Hebrews 10:23

In Denial of Self

Give Me Strength to Pour Myself Out

Whoever wants to become great among you
must be your servant, and whoever wants to be
first among you must be your slave; just as the
Son of Man did not come to be served, but to
serve, and to give His life—a ransom for many.

Matthew 20:26-28

Everything is permissible," but not everything is helpful. "Everything is permissible," but not everything builds up. No one should seek his own good, but the good of the other person.

1 Corinthians 10:23-24

For where envy and selfish ambition exist, there is disorder and every kind of evil. But the wisdom from above is first pure, then peace-loving, gentle, compliant, full of mercy and good fruits, without favoritism and hypocrisy. And the fruit of righteousness is sown in peace by those who make peace.

James 3:16-18

Carry one another's burdens; in this way you will fulfill the law of Christ.

Galatians 6:2

Just as you want others to do for you, do the same for them.

Luke 6:31

Parenthood comes with a lot of new jobs. I guess you know that by now. *But a lot of times, you're not going to feel like taking on these restrictive responsibilities. That's when we learn to let our feelings take a back seat.*

The person who sows sparingly will also reap sparingly, and the person who sows generously will also reap generously. Each person should do as he has decided in his heart—not out of regret or out of necessity, for God loves a cheerful giver. And God is able to make every grace overflow to you, so that in every way, always having everything you need, you may excel in every good work.

2 Corinthians 9:6-8

Don't neglect to do good and to share, for God is pleased with such sacrifices.

Hebrews 13:16

A generous person will be enriched.

Proverbs 11:25

All of you should be like-minded and sympathetic, should love believers, and be compassionate and humble, not paying back evil for evil or insult for insult but, on the contrary, giving a blessing, since you were called for this, so that you can inherit a blessing.

1 Peter 3:8-9

Do not grow weary in doing good.

2 Thessalonians 3:13

And be kind and compassionate to one another, forgiving one another, just as God also forgave you in Christ.

Ephesians 4:32

Therefore, God's chosen ones, holy and loved, put on heartfelt compassion, kindness, humility, gentleness, and patience, accepting one another and forgiving one another if anyone has a complaint against another.

Just as the Lord has forgiven you, so also you must forgive.

Above all, put on love—the perfect bond of unity. And let the peace of the Messiah, to which you were also called in one body, control your hearts. Be thankful.

Colossians 3:12-15

You'll grow closer to each other as you move farther away from yourself.
Giving when it really costs you is one of the best ways to draw near to the heart of God. The rich blessings of denying yourself just can't be denied.

Now may the God of peace, who brought up from the dead our Lord Jesus—the great Shepherd of the sheep—with the blood of the everlasting covenant, equip you with all that is good to do His will, working in us what is pleasing in His sight, through Jesus Christ, to whom be glory forever and ever. Amen.

Hebrews 13:20-21

Do nothing out of rivalry or conceit, but in humility consider others as more important than yourselves.

Philippians 2:3

May the Lord cause you to increase and overflow with love for one another and for everyone.

1 Thessalonians 3:12

In and Out of Patience

This Is Not the Easiest Job in the World

Love is patient; love is kind. Love does not envy; is not boastful; is not conceited; does not act improperly; is not selfish; is not provoked; does not keep a record of wrongs; finds no joy in unrighteousness, but rejoices in the truth; bears all things, believes all things, hopes all things, endures all things.

1 Corinthians 13:4-7

I said, "If only I had wings like a dove!
I would fly away and find rest. How far away
I would flee; I would stay in the wilderness.
I would hurry to my shelter from the raging
wind and the storm.". . . Cast your burden on
the LORD, and He will support you; He will
never allow the righteous to be shaken.

Psalm 55:6-8, 22

Take the prophets who spoke in the Lord's
name as an example of suffering and patience.
See, we count as blessed those who have
endured. You have heard of Job's endurance
and have seen the outcome from the Lord:
the Lord is very compassionate and merciful.

James 5:10-11

As for me, I will watch for the LORD; I will
wait for the God who saves me. My God will
hear me.

Micah 7:7

A patient person shows great understanding.

Proverbs 14:29

Patience is learned best at home, where it has real life to exercise it.

Calm nerves and a cool temper are created over spilled milk and sobbing babies. But the patience you earn now will pay dividends for a lifetime.

Therefore strengthen your tired hands and weakened knees, and make straight paths for your feet, so that what is lame may not be dislocated, but healed instead.

Hebrews 12:12-13

Do everything without grumbling and arguing, so that you may be blameless and pure, children of God who are faultless in a crooked and perverted generation, among whom you shine like stars in the world.

Philippians 2:14-15

Be alert, stand firm in the faith, be brave and strong. Your every action must be done with love.

1 Corinthians 16:13

Who perceives his unintentional sins? Cleanse me from my hidden faults. Moreover, keep Your servant from willful sins; do not let them rule over me. Then I will be innocent, and cleansed from blatant rebellion. May the words of my mouth and the meditation of my heart be acceptable to You, O LORD, my rock and my Redeemer.

Psalm 19:12-14

I have been crucified with Christ; and I no longer live, but Christ lives in me. The life I now live in the flesh, I live by faith in the Son of God, who loved me and gave Himself for me.

Galatians 2:19-20

Make your own attitude that of Christ Jesus, who, existing in the form of God, did not consider equality with God as something to be used for His own advantage.

Instead He emptied Himself by assuming the form of a slave, taking on the likeness of men. And when He had come as a man in His external form, He humbled Himself by becoming obedient to the point of death—even to death on a cross.

Philippians 2:5-8

In and Out of Patience

Like everything else in life, winning at patience comes in surrendering to God. *Pray about it. Ask God to steady your wits when you feel yourself coming unglued. He'll always be there to help you, for His patience knows no end.*

Now we have this treasure in clay jars, so that this extraordinary power may be from God and not from us.

2 Corinthians 4:7

But the fruit of the Spirit is love, joy, peace, patience, kindness, goodness, faith, gentleness, self-control. Against such things there is no law.

Galatians 5:22-23

Do not lack diligence; be fervent in spirit; serve the Lord. Rejoice in hope; be patient in affliction; be persistent in prayer.

Romans 12:11-12

Comfort the discouraged, help the weak, be patient with everyone.

1 Thessalonians 5:14

Promises to Keep

You've been focusing on this moment for so many months. And it really is special, isn't it? Things that used to seem so important sort of melt into nothing when that soft face is next to yours, when those eyes blink in your direction, when those wet fingers curl around yours.

Yet the love you feel for this little one pales in comparison to the love your Father has for him, for her. Bundle up every hope you dream for this child, and your Father's are greater still. With Him, your baby will have everything.

Making a Firm Commitment

God Is Coming First in Our Home

Take to heart all these words I am giving as a warning to you today, so that you may command your children to carefully follow all the words of this law. For they are not meaningless words to you but they are your life.

Deuteronomy 32:46-47

Come, children, listen to me; I will teach you the fear of the LORD.

Psalm 34:11

Do not despise the LORD's instruction, my son, and do not loathe His discipline; for the Lord disciplines the one He loves, just as a father, the son he delights in.

Proverbs 3:11-12

No discipline seems enjoyable at the time, but painful. Later on, however, it yields the fruit of peace and righteousness to those who have been trained by it.

Hebrews 12:11

My little children, I am writing you these things so that you may not sin. But if anyone does sin, we have an advocate with the Father— Jesus Christ the righteous One. He Himself is the propitiation for our sins, and not only for ours, but also for those of the whole world.

1 John 2:1-2

The best way to put your faith into action is to keep your nose in the Word. *You've been doing it all through this book, and you'll do it the rest of your life. Teach the Bible to your children, and they'll never get a wrong steer.*

We have not received the spirit of the world, but the Spirit who is from God, in order to know what has been freely given to us by God.

1 Corinthians 2:12

All Scripture is inspired by God and is profitable for teaching, for rebuking, for correcting, for training in righteousness.

2 Timothy 3:16

When you walk here and there, they will guide you; when you lie down, they will watch over you; when you wake up, they will talk to you. For a commandment is a lamp, teaching is a light, and corrective instructions are the way to life.

Proverbs 6:22-23

Therefore, get your minds ready for action, being self-disciplined, and set your hope completely on the grace to be brought to you at the revelation of Jesus Christ. As obedient children, do not be conformed to the desires of your former ignorance but, as the One who called you is holy, you also are to be holy in all your conduct; for it is written, "Be holy, because I am holy."

1 Peter 1:13-16

Commit your activities to the LORD and your plans will be achieved.

Proverbs 16:3

Promises to Keep

I pray that the God of our Lord Jesus Christ, the glorious Father, would give you a spirit of wisdom and revelation in the knowledge of Him. I pray that the eyes of your heart may be enlightened so you may know what is the hope of His calling, what are the glorious riches of His inheritance among the saints, and what is the immeasurable greatness of His power to us who believe, according to the working of His vast strength.

Ephesians 1:17-19

To be like Him, your child needs to learn both the fear and the love of God.
Some people are all frowns. Some are all smiles. But you'll find that your children grow best when both faces have their place in your parenting.

There are thorns and snares on the path of the crooked; the one who guards himself stays far from them. Teach a youth about the way he should go; even when he is old he will not depart from it.

Proverbs 22:5-6

Discipline your son, and he will give you comfort; he will also give you delight.

Proverbs 29:17

Then we will no longer be little children, tossed by the waves and blown around by every wind of teaching, by human cunning with cleverness in the techniques of deceit. But speaking the truth in love, let us grow in every way into Him who is the head—Christ.

Ephesians 4:14-15

Giving a Good Name

May We Be Known for Knowing God

I pray that you, being rooted and firmly established in love, may be able to comprehend with all the saints what is the breadth and width, height and depth, and to know the Messiah's love that surpasses knowledge, so you may be filled with all the fullness of God.

Ephesians 3:17-19

A good name is better than fine perfume.

Ecclesiastes 7:1

A good name is to be chosen over great wealth; favor is better than silver and gold.

Proverbs 22:1

The LORD will grant you a blessing on your storehouses and on everything you do; He will bless you in the land the LORD your God is giving you. The LORD will establish you as His holy people, as He swore to you, if you obey the commands of the LORD your God and walk in His ways. Then all the peoples of the earth will see that you are called by the LORD's name, and they will stand in awe of you.

Deuteronomy 28:8-10

When he calls out to Me, I will answer him; I will be with him in trouble. I will rescue him and give him honor. I will satisfy him with a long life and show him My salvation.

Psalm 91:15-16

The best thing you can do for your children is to lead them to the Lord.

Many people will have many expectations for what your children should be like. Want nothing more than that they will be like their Father.

If your heart is wise, my heart will indeed rejoice. My innermost being will cheer when your lips say what is right. Don't be jealous of sinners; instead, always fear the Lord. For then you will have a future, and your hope will never fade.

Proverbs 23:15-18

Your eyes will see your Teacher, and whenever you turn to the right or to the left, your ears will hear this command behind you: "This is the way. Walk in it."

Isaiah 30:20-21

I have no greater joy than this: to hear that my children are walking in the truth.

3 John 4

Giving a Good Name

We have confidence in the Lord about you,
that you are doing and will do what we command. May the Lord direct your hearts to
God's love and Christ's endurance.

2 Thessalonians 3:4-5

Don't work for the food that perishes but for
the food that lasts for eternal life, which the
Son of Man will give you, because on Him
God the Father has set His seal of approval.

John 6:27

Little children, we must not love in word or
speech, but in deed and truth.

1 John 3:18

My people, hear my instruction; listen to what I say. I will declare wise sayings; I will speak mysteries from the past—things we have heard and known and that our fathers have passed down to us. We must not hide them from their children, but must tell a future generation the praises of the LORD, His might, and the wonderful works He has performed.... so that a future generation—children yet to be born—might know. They were to rise and tell their children so that they might put their confidence in God and not forget God's works, but keep His commandments.

Psalm 78:1-4, 6-7

Giving a Good Name

Your name sounds best when you and God are spoken in the same sentence. *When people look at you and your family, pray that they will see you as someone whose love for each other is only matched by your love for God.*

Not to us, LORD, not to us, but to Your name give glory because of Your faithful love, because of Your truth.

Psalm 115:1

Yes, LORD, we wait for You in the path of Your judgments. Our desire is for Your name and renown. . . . LORD, our God, other lords than You have ruled over us, but Your name alone we remember.

Isaiah 26:8, 13

Ascribe to the LORD, families of the peoples, ascribe to the LORD glory and strength. Ascribe to the LORD the glory of His name; bring an offering and enter His courts. Worship the LORD in His holy majesty.

Psalm 96:7-9

Building a Strong Heritage

For Him, For Our Future, Forever

Children, obey your parents in the Lord, because this is right. Honor your father and mother—which is the first commandment with a promise—that it may go well with you and that you may have a long life in the land.

Ephesians 6:1-3

Happy is the man who fears the LORD,
taking great delight in His commandments.
His descendants will be powerful in the land;
the generation of the upright will be blessed.

Psalm 112:1-2

No weapon formed against you will succeed,
and you will refute any accusation raised against
you in court. This is the heritage of the LORD's
servants, and their righteousness is from Me,"
declares the LORD.

Isaiah 54:17

Tell your children about it, and let your children tell their children, and their children the
next generation.

Joel 1:3

Go around Zion, encircle it; count its towers,
note its ramparts; tour its citadels so that you
can tell a future generation: "This God, our God
forever and ever—He will lead us eternally."

Psalm 48:12-14

Seek the kingdom of God, and He will take care of your corner of the world. *Learn how to see your future through the eyes of today. The inheritance you hand down to your children will be given out a day at a time.*

Who is the person who fears the LORD? He will show him the way he should choose. He will live a good life, and his descendants will inherit the land.

Psalm 25:12-13

O Lord, let Your ear be attentive to the prayer of Your servant and to the prayer of Your servants who delight in revering Your name.

Nehemiah 1:11

I know that all God accomplishes will last forever. Nothing can be added to it, and nothing can be taken away from it. God works so people may stand in awe of Him.

Ecclesiastes 3:14

Know that Yahweh your God is God, the faithful God who keeps covenant loyalty to a thousandth generation for those who love Him and keep His commandments.

Deuteronomy 7:9

Choose life so that you and your descendants may live, love the LORD your God, obey Him, and remain faithful to Him.

Deuteronomy 30:19-20

I have Your decrees as a heritage forever; indeed, they are the joy of my heart.

Psalm 119:111

You, LORD, are enthroned forever; Your fame endures to all generations. . . .

Long ago You established the earth, and the heavens are the work of Your hands. They will perish, but You will endure; all of them will wear out like clothing. You will change them like a garment, and they will pass away.

But You are the same, and Your years will never end. Your servants' children will dwell securely, and their offspring will be established before You.

Psalm 102:12, 25-28

You have an incredible future ahead of you. Let your child follow in its wake. *When your faith is more than talk, when it's lived out in the flesh and blood of real life, your children will see it, know it, and learn to love it.*

You have given a heritage to those who fear Your name.

Psalm 61:5

Watch the blameless and observe the upright, for the man of peace will have a future.

Psalm 37:37

My son, don't forget my teaching, but let your heart keep my commands; for they will bring you many days, a full life, and well-being. Never let loyalty and faithfulness leave you. Tie them around your neck; write them on the tablet of your heart. Then you will find favor and high regard in the sight of God and man.

Proverbs 3:1-4

Sharing a Sure Salvation

Nothing Is More Important than This

God loved the world in this way: He gave His One and Only Son, so that everyone who believes in Him will not perish but have eternal life. For God did not send His Son into the world that He might judge the world, but that the world might be saved through Him.

John 3:16-17

Love consists in this: not that we loved God, but that He loved us and sent His Son to be the propitiation for our sins.

1 John 4:10

This saying is trustworthy and deserving of full acceptance: "Christ Jesus came into the world to save sinners"—and I am the worst of them. But I received mercy because of this, so that in me, the worst of them, Christ Jesus might demonstrate the utmost patience.

1 Timothy 1:15-16

Whoever confesses that Jesus is the Son of God—God remains in him and he in God.

1 John 4:15

There is salvation in no one else, for there is no other name under heaven given to people by which we must be saved.

Acts 4:12

How will we escape if we neglect such a great salvation?

Hebrews 2:3

We wouldn't have required such love if it weren't for a big problem we all have. *It would be nice to think otherwise, but even that precious new baby in your arms has been born hopelessly lost in sin. We all need God's grace.*

The LORD's hand is not too short to save, and His ear is not too deaf to hear. But your iniquities have built barriers between you and your God, and your sins have made Him hide His face from you so that He does not listen.

Isaiah 59:1-2

Your guilty acts have diverted these things from you. Your sins have withheld the bounty from you.

Jeremiah 5:25

By nature we were children under wrath, as the others were also. But God, who is abundant in mercy, because of His great love that He had for us, made us alive with the Messiah even though we were dead in trespasses.

Ephesians 2:3-5

While we were still helpless, at the appointed moment, Christ died for the ungodly. For rarely will someone die for a just person—though for a good person perhaps someone might even dare to die. But God proves His own love for us in that while we were still sinners Christ died for us! . . . For if, while we were enemies, we were reconciled to God through the death of His Son, then how much more, having been reconciled, will we be saved by His life!

Romans 5:6-8, 10

Therefore, since we have been declared righteous by faith, we have peace with God through our Lord Jesus Christ.

Romans 5:1

This is the message of faith that we proclaim: if you confess with your mouth, "Jesus is Lord," and believe in your heart that God raised Him from the dead, you will be saved.

With the heart one believes, resulting in righteousness, and with the mouth one confesses, resulting in salvation.

Now the Scripture says, "No one who believes on Him will be put to shame," for there is no distinction between Jew and Greek, since the same Lord of all is rich to all who call on Him. For "everyone who calls on the name of the Lord will be saved."

Romans 10:8-13

Has Jesus Christ become your Savior and Lord? What else really matters?

He's promised to come near every one of us who calls to Him. Be sure that's you. And start early whispering to your child about what this means.

What then are we to say about these things? If God is for us, who is against us? He did not even spare His own Son, but offered Him up for us all; how will He not also with Him grant us everything?

Romans 8:31-32

For by grace you are saved through faith, and this is not from yourselves; it is God's gift—not from works, so that no one can boast.

Ephesians 2:8-9

But to all who did receive Him, He gave them the right to be children of God, to those who believe in His name, who were born, not of blood, or of the will of the flesh, or of the will of man, but of God.

John 1:12-13

*Look for these other Bible Promise books
to give to the special people in your life.*

**Bible Promises
for Mom**
0-8054-2732-5

**Bible Promises
for Dad**
0-8054-2733-3

**Bible Promises
for My Teacher**
0-8054-2734-1

**Bible Promises
for the Graduate**
0-8054-2741-4

**Bible Promises
for New Believers**
0-8054-2742-2

**Bible Promises
for New Parents**
0-8054-2738-4

**Bible Promises
for Kids**
0-8054-2740-6

**Bible Promises
for Teens**
0-8054-2739-2